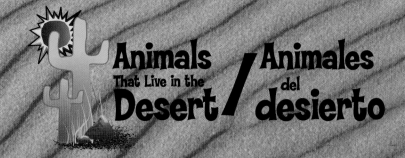

Animals That Live in the Desert / Animales del desierto

Jackrabbits/ Liebres americanas

JoAnn Early Macken

Reading consultant/Consultora de lectura:
Susan Nations, M. Ed., author, literacy coach,
consultant/autora, tutora de alfabetización, consultora

Please visit our web site at: www.earlyliteracy.cc
For a free color catalog describing Weekly Reader® Early Learning Library's list
of high-quality books, call 1-877-445-5824 (USA) or 1-800-387-3178 (Canada).
Weekly Reader® Early Learning Library's fax: (414) 336-0164.

Library of Congress Cataloging-in-Publication Data available upon request from publisher.
Fax (414) 336-0157 for the attention of the Publishing Records Department.

ISBN 0-8368-4842-X (lib. bdg.)
ISBN 0-8368-4849-7 (softcover)

This edition first published in 2006 by
Weekly Reader® Early Learning Library
A Member of the WRC Media Family of Companies
330 West Olive Street, Suite 100
Milwaukee, WI 53212 USA

Art direction: Tammy West
Cover design and page layout: Kami Koenig
Picture research: Diane Laska-Swanke
Translators: Tatiana Acosta and Guillermo Gutiérrez

Picture credits: Cover, p. 21 © John and Barbara Gerlach/Visuals Unlimited;
p. 5 © James P. Rowan; p. 7 © Rick and Nora Bowers/Visuals Unlimited;
p. 9 © Richard Day/Daybreak Imagery; p. 11 © Corel; p. 13 © Tom and
Pat Leeson; pp. 15, 17 © Michael H. Francis; p. 19 © Jeff Foott/naturepl.com

Printed in the United States of America

1 2 3 4 5 6 7 8 9 09 08 07 06 05

Note to Educators and Parents

Reading is such an exciting adventure for young children! They are beginning to integrate their oral language skills with written language. To encourage children along the path to early literacy, books must be colorful, engaging, and interesting; they should invite the young reader to explore both the print and the pictures.

Animals That Live in the Desert is a new series designed to help children read about creatures that make their homes in dry places. Each book explains where a different desert animal lives, what it eats, and how it adapts to its arid environment.

Each book is specially designed to support the young reader in the reading process. The familiar topics are appealing to young children and invite them to read — and reread — again and again. The full-color photographs and enhanced text further support the student during the reading process.

In addition to serving as wonderful picture books in schools, libraries, homes, and other places where children learn to love reading, these books are specifically intended to be read within an instructional guided reading group. This small group setting allows beginning readers to work with a fluent adult model as they make meaning from the text. After children develop fluency with the text and content, the book can be read independently. Children and adults alike will find these books supportive, engaging, and fun!

— Susan Nations, M.Ed., author, literacy coach,
and consultant in literacy development

Nota para los maestros y los padres

¡Leer es una aventura tan emocionante para los niños pequeños! A esta edad están comenzando a integrar su manejo del lenguaje oral con el lenguaje escrito. Para animar a los niños en el camino de la lectura incipiente, los libros deben ser coloridos, estimulantes e interesantes; deben invitar a los jóvenes lectores a explorar la letra impresa y las ilustraciones.

Animales del desierto es una nueva colección diseñada para que los niños lean textos sobre animales que viven en lugares muy secos. Cada libro explica dónde vive un animal del desierto, qué come y cómo se adapta a su árido medio ambiente.

Cada libro está especialmente diseñado para ayudar a los jóvenes lectores en el proceso de lectura. Los temas familiares llaman la atención de los niños y los invitan a leer —y releer— una y otra vez. Las fotografías a todo color y el tamaño de la letra ayudan aún más al estudiante en el proceso de lectura.

Además de servir como maravillosos libros ilustrados en escuelas, bibliotecas, hogares y otros lugares donde los niños aprenden a amar la lectura, estos libros han sido especialmente concebidos para ser leídos en un grupo de lectura guiada. Este contexto permite que los lectores incipientes trabajen con un adulto que domina la lectura mientras van determinando el significado del texto. Una vez que los niños dominan el texto y el contenido, el libro puede ser leído de manera independiente. ¡Estos libros les resultarán útiles, estimulantes y divertidos a niños y a adultos por igual!

— Susan Nations, M.Ed., autora/tutora de alfabetización/
consultora de desarrollo de la lectura

Jackrabbits are hares. Hares are longer and thinner than rabbits. Hares have long ears and long, strong hind legs.

- - - - - - - - - - - - - - -

Las liebres americanas son un tipo de liebre. Las liebres son más largas y delgadas que los conejos. Las liebres tienen orejas largas y patas traseras largas y fuertes.

ear/
oreja

hind leg/
pata trasera

5

In hot weather, they lift their ears to cool off. In cold weather, they keep their ears down to stay warm. They can turn their ears to hear better.

Cuando hace calor, las liebres americanas levantan las orejas para refrescarse. Cuando hace frío, las agachan para calentarse. Para oír mejor, pueden hacerlas girar.

7

Jackrabbits are gray, brown, and white. Their colors blend into the desert.

Las liebres americanas son grises, color café y blancas. Esos colores son difíciles de ver en el desierto.

Some jackrabbits have black tips on their ears. They have black stripes on their tails.

Algunas liebres americanas tienen la punta de las orejas negra, y una franja negra en la cola.

ear/
oreja

tail/
cola

11

Jackrabbits are active at night.
They eat grass, leaves, and twigs.
In the desert, they even eat cacti!

- - - - - - - - - - - - -

Las liebres americanas están
activas por la noche. Comen
hierba, hojas y ramitas. ¡En el
desierto, llegan a comerse los
cactus!

They eat in open areas. They watch out for hawks and owls. They watch out for coyotes.

- - - - - - - - - - - - - -

Las liebres americanas comen en áreas abiertas. Vigilan que no haya halcones ni búhos. Vigilan que no haya coyotes.

14

They run fast to get away from predators. They leap on their long, strong legs.

Para escapar de los depredadores, las liebres americanas corren muy deprisa. Brincan con sus patas largas y fuertes.

During the day, they rest in the shade. They may rest under bushes. They may rest in shallow holes they dig in the ground.

Durante el día, las liebres americanas descansan a la sombra. Pueden descansar bajo unos arbustos. Pueden descansar en agujeros poco profundos que excavan en el suelo.

Baby jackrabbits are born with soft fur. Their eyes are open. Their mother feeds them milk at first. In about one month, they can be on their own.

- - - - - - - - - - - - - -

Las crías de liebre americana tienen un pelo suave al nacer. Nacen con los ojos abiertos. Al principio, la madre las alimenta con leche. Un mes después, ya pueden sobrevivir solas.

GLOSSARY

cacti — desert plants with thick stems and spiny leaves

desert — a very dry area

hind — back

leap — to jump

predators — animals that eat other animals

GLOSARIO

brincar — saltar

cactus — plantas del desierto de tallos gruesos y hojas espinosas

depredadores — animales que se comen a otros animales

desierto — un área muy seca

trasera — de atrás

FOR MORE INFORMATION/ MÁS INFORMACIÓN

BOOKS IN ENGLISH

Alejandro's Gift. Richard E. Albert (Chronicle)

Jackrabbits. Emily Rose Townsend (Pebble Books)

LIBROS EN ESPAÑOL

I Live in the Desert/Vivo en el desierto. Gini Holland (Weekly
  Reader Early Learning Library)

The Tortoise and the Jackrabbit/La Tortuga y la Liebre. Susan
  Lowell (Rising Moon Books)

INDEX

ÍNDICE

ABOUT THE AUTHOR

JoAnn Early Macken is the author of two rhyming picture books, *Sing-Along Song* and *Cats on Judy*, and many other nonfiction books for beginning readers. Her poems have appeared in several children's magazines. A graduate of the M.F.A. in Writing for Children and Young Adults program at Vermont College, she lives in Wisconsin with her husband and their two sons. Visit her Web site at www.joannmacken.com.

INFORMACIÓN SOBRE LA AUTORA

JoAnn Early Macken ha escrito dos libros de rimas con ilustraciones, *Sing-Along Song* y *Cats on Judy*, y muchos otros libros de no ficción para lectores incipientes. Sus poemas han sido publicados en varias revistas infantiles. JoAnn se graduó en el programa M.F.A. de Escritura para Niños y Jóvenes de Vermont College. Vive en Wisconsin con su esposo y sus dos hijos. Puedes visitar su página web: www.joannmacken.com